Deportation
Its Meaning And Menace

by

Alexander Berkman And Emma Goldman

ABOUT THE AUTHOR

Born in Vilna (modern-day Vilnius, Lithuania), Berkman entered the turbulent world of the labour movement and anarchist thought as soon as he arrived in the United States in 1888. His attempt to kill Carnegie Steel president Henry Clay Frick in 1892 during the Homestead Steel Strike earned him notoriety. During his fourteen years in prison, Berkman wrote a great deal. His "Prison Memoirs of an Anarchist" examined the inequalities in the American legal system as well as his personal experiences. Berkman had a long-lasting influence on the movement because of his commitment to anarchism and his criticism of the capitalist system.

Born in Kovno, which is now Kaunas, Lithuania, Goldman came to the United States in 1885. Known as "Red Emma," she became well-known for her persuasive writing and speaking, supporting a variety of causes like as free speech, women's emancipation, and workers' rights. Goldman, a major player in the labor movement, was crucial to the events of the Haymarket Affair in 1886. Her works and talks, such as "Anarchism and Other Essays," struck a chord with readers and advocated for anarchism as a way to attain personal autonomy and social justice.

CONTENTS

INTRODUCTION

With pencil and scraps of paper concealed behind the persons of friends who had come to say good-bye at the Ellis Island Deportation Station, Alexander Berkman hastily scribbled the last lines of this pamphlet.

I think it is the best introduction to this pamphlet to say that before its writing was finished the rulers of America began deporting men directly and obviously for the offense of *striking against the industrial owners of America.*

The "Red Ark" is gone. In the darkness of early morning it slipped away, leaving behind many wives and children destitute of support. They were denied even the knowledge of the sailing of the ship, denied the right of farewell to the husbands and fathers they may never see again. After the boat was gone, women and children came to the dock to visit the prisoners, bringing such little comforts as are known to the working class, seedy overcoats for the Russian winter, cheap gloves and odds and ends of food. They were told that the ship was gone. The refined cruelty of the thing was too much for them; they stormed the ferry-house, broke a window, screamed and cried, and were driven away by soldiers.

The "Red Ark" will loom big in American history. It is the first picturesque incident of the beginning effort of the War Millionaires to crush the soul of America and insure the safety of the dollars they have looted over the graves of Europe and through the deaths of the quarter million soldier boys whom American mothers now mourn.

Yes, the "Red Ark" will go into history. Alexander Berkman and Emma Goldman whom the screaming harlots of the yellow press have chosen to call the "leaders" of those whose distinction is that they have no leaders, are more fortunate than otherwise. Berkman and Goldman have been deported as "Russians." They were born in Russia, but they did their thirty years' work of enlightenment in this, our America. I think they are therefore Americans, in the best sense, and the best of Americans. They fought for the elementary rights of men, here in our country when others of us were afraid to speak, or would not pay the price. In all the leading cities of this land, they have contributed to the intellectual life of the younger, aspiring generation. I venture to say that there is hardly a liberal in the United States whose life has not been influenced directly or indirectly and made better, by Alexander Berkman and Emma Goldman.

Alexander Berkman spent in American prisons more years than I like to remember. He did it deliberately. He did it for the welfare of men, and the American portion of mankind. He never hesitated to offer his life for his brother. I recall a picture; it is in Russia. We were gathered in Moscow. It looked as though the Revolution were going to its death. Everywhere the Soviet armies were retreating, the masses were sinking into despair, the German working class was not rising in rebellion as we had hoped, the Austrians likewise; the White Terror was raising its head throughout Russia. A pallid girl, a Russian-American immigrant returned to her native country, held in her hand the bulletin of the day's news. "A hundred Alexander Berkmans distributed throughout Europe at this time, and the history of Europe would be different!" she exclaimed.

Berkman wrote a book, "Prison Memoirs of an Anarchist," which is one of America's vital literary products. It won for him the admiration of such intellectuals here as had the courage to admire.

The "intellectuals" for the most part did not bid Emma Goldman and Alexander Berkman good-bye. Most of those who dared to visit the passengers of the "Red Ark" in their Ellis Island prison were young men and women of the working class. That is as it should be. It is in the working class where Goldman and Berkman's brave work will find the growth that will count. American plutocracy knew this. That is why American plutocracy deported Alexander Berkman and Emma Goldman.

This pamphlet is the "good-bye message" of Alexander Berkman and Emma Goldman; and I think it is in spirit the message of all the passengers of the "Red Ark." As such it appears first in this form and will appear later in history. Read it and keep it for the future.

Robert Minor.

DEPORTATION—Its Meaning and Menace

The war is over, but peace there is not. On a score of fronts human slaughter is going on as before; men, women, and children are dying by the hundred thousands because of the blockade of Russia; the "small nations" are still under the iron heel of the foreign oppressor; Ireland, India, Egypt, Persia, Korea, and numerous other peoples, are being decimated and exploited even more ruthlessly than before the advent of the Great Prophet of World Democracy; "self-determination" has become a by-word, nay, a crime, and world-wide imperialism has gotten a strangle hold upon humanity.

What, then, has the Great War accomplished? To what purpose the sacrifice of millions of human lives, the unnamable loss in blood and treasure? What, especially, has happened in these United States?

Fresh in mind are still the wonderful promises made in behalf of the War. It was to be the *last* war, a holy crusade of liberty against tyranny, a war upon all wars that was to sweep the earth clear of oppression and misery, and make the world safe for true democracy.

As with a sacred fire burned the heart of mankind. What soul so small, what human so low, not to be inspired by the glorious shibboleth of liberty and well-being for all! A tornado of social enthusiasm, a new-born world consciousness, swept the United States. The people were aflame with a new faith; they would slay the Dragon of Despotism, and conquer the world for democracy.

True, it was but yesterday their sovereign will registered a mighty protest against human slaughter and bloodshed. With a magnificent majority they had voted not to participate in the foreign War, not to become entangled in the treacherous schemes of European despotisms. Triumphantly they had elected as President of the United States the man who "kept them out of the war" that he might still keep them out of it.

Then suddenly, almost over night, came the change. From Wall Street sounded the bugle ordering the retreat of Humanity. Its echo reverberated in Washington, and thence throughout the whole country. There began a campaign of war publicity that roused the tiger in man and fed his lust for blood and vengeance. The quiet, phlegmatic German was transformed into the "Vicious Hun," and made the villain of the wildest stories of "enemy" atrocities and outrages. The nation-wide propaganda of hatred, persecution, and intolerance carried its subtle poison into the hearts of the obscurest hamlet, and the minds of the people were systematically confused and perverted by rivers of printer's ink. The conscience of America, wanting peace, was stifled in the folds of the national emblem, and its voice drowned by the martial beat of a thousand war drums.

Here and there a note of protest was heard. Radicals of various political and social faiths — Anarchists, Socialists, I. W. Ws., some pacifists, conscientious objectors, and other anti-militarists — sought to stem the tide of the war hysteria. They pointed out that the people of the United States had no interest in the European War. That this country, because of its geographical location and natural advantages, was beyond all danger of invasion. They showed that the War was the result of European over-preparedness for war, aggravated by a crisis in capitalist competition, old monarchical rivalries and ambitions of super-despotic rulers. The peoples of Europe, the radicals emphasized, had neither say nor interest in the war: they were the sheep led to slaughter on the altar of Mammon contending against Baal. America's great humanitarian mission, the war protestants insisted, was to keep out of the war, and use its potent influence and compelling economic and financial power to terminate the European slaughter and bring peace to the bleeding nations of the old world.

But these voices of sanity and judgment were lost in the storm of unloosed war passions. The brave men and women that dared to speak in behalf of peace and humanity, that had the surpassing integrity of remaining true to themselves and to their ideals, with the courage of facing danger and death for conscience sake — these, the truest friends of Man, had to bear the cross of Golgotha, as did the Nazarene of yore, as the lovers of humanity have done all through the centuries of human progress. The jail and lynch law for them; execution and persecution by their contemporaries. But if it be true that history repeats itself, surely these political "criminals" of today will be hailed tomorrow as martyrs and pioneers.

The popular war hysteria was roused and especially successfully cultivated by the alleged progressive, "intellectual" element in the United States. Their notoriously overwhelming self-esteem and vanity had been subtly flattered by their fellow-intellectual, the college professor become President. This American *intelligentzia* inclusive of a good many quite unintelligent suffragettes, was the real "balance of power" in the re-election of Woodrow Wilson. The silken cord (occasionally golden in spots) of mutual interest that bound the President and the intellectual element ultimately proved much stronger at their end than at his. The feeling of gratitude is always more potent with the giver than with the recipient. Howbeit the "liberals", the "radicals", were devoted heart and soul to the professor,—they stood solidly behind the President, to use their own intellectually expressive phrase.

Shame upon the mighty power of the human mind! It was the "radical intellectuals" who, as a class, turned traitors to the best interests of humanity, perverted their calling and traditions, and became the bloodiest canines of Mars. With a power of sophistry that the Greek masters of false logic never matched, they cited history, philosophy, science—aye, they called their very Christ to witness that the killing of man by man is a most worthy and respectable occupation, indeed a very Christian institution, and that wholesale human slaughter, if properly directed and successfully conducted, is a very necessary evolutionary factor, a great blessing in disguise.

It was this "intellectual" element that by perversion of the human mind turned a peace-demanding people into a war-mad mob. The popular refusal to volunteer for Service was hailed by them as a universal demand for military draft as "the most democratic expression of a free citizenship." Forced service became in their interpretation "equality of contribution for rich and poor alike." The protest of one's conscience against killing was branded by them as high treason, and even mere disagreement regarding the causes of the war, or the slightest criticism of the administration, was condemned as disloyalty and pro-Germanism. Every expression of humanity, of social sympathy, and understanding was cried down with a Babel of high phrases, in which "patriotism" and "democracy" competed in volume. Oh, the tragedy of the human mind that absorbs fine words and empty phrases, and is deaf to motives and blind to deeds!

Yet there lacked unanimity in the strenuously cultivated war demand. There was no popular enthusiasm for American participation in the European holocaust. Mothers protested against their children being torn from the home hearth; fathers hid their young sons. The spirit of discontent was abroad. The Government had to resort to drastic methods: the hand of white terror was lifted in Washington. Again we raised our voices to warn the people,—we, the revolutionists of various social views who remained true to our ideal of human brotherhood and proletarian solidarity. We pointed out that the masses of the world had nothing to gain and everything to lose by war; that the chief sufferers of every war were the workers, and that they were being used as mere pawns in the game of international diplomacy and imperialist capitalism. We reminded the toilers that they alone possessed the power to wage war or make peace, and that they—as the creators of the world's wealth—were the true arbiters of the fate of humanity. Their mission, we reiterated, is to secure peace on earth, and the product of labor to the producers.

Emphatically we warned the people of America against the policy of suppression by the enactment of special legislation. Alleged war necessity was being used—we asserted—to incorporate in the statute books new laws and new legal principles that would remain operative *after* the war, and be effective for the continued prohibition of governmentally unapproved thoughts and views. The practice of stifling and choking free speech and press, established and tolerated during the war, sets a most dangerous precedent for after-war days. The principle of such outrages upon liberty once introduced, it will require a long and arduous struggle to win back the liberties lost. "Eternal vigilance is the price of liberty." Thus we argued.

Here again the "intellectuals" and radicals of chameleon hue hastened to the rescue of the forces of reaction. We were scoffed at, our "vain fears" ridiculed. It was all for the best interests of the country—the sophists protested—for the greater security and glory of Democracy.

II

Now reaction is in full swing. The actual reality is even darker than our worst predictions. Liberty is dead, and white terror on top dominates the country. Free speech is a thing of the past. Not a city in the whole wide land but that forbids the least expression of an unpopular opinion. It is descriptive of the whole situation that after thirty years' activity in New York, we are unable—upon our return from prison—to secure any hall, large or small, to lecture even on the subject of prison life or to speak on the question of amnesty for political and industrial prisoners. The doors of every meeting place are closed to us, as well as to other revolutionists, by order of the powers that be.

Free press has been abolished, and every radical paper that dares speak out, is summarily suppressed. Raids of public gatherings, of offices, and private dwelling places, accomplished with utmost brutality and uncalled for violence, are of daily occurrence throughout the United States. The headquarters of Anarchists, of Socialists, of I. W. Ws., of the Union of Russian Workers, and numerous other progressive and educational organizations, have been raided by the local police and Federal agents in practically every city of this country. Men and women are beaten up indiscriminately, fearfully clubbed and blackjacked without any provocation, frequently to be released afterwards because no offence whatever could be charged against them. Books and whole libraries of "radical centers" are confiscated, even text books of arithmetic or geography torn to shreds, furniture destroyed, pianos and victrolas smashed to kindling wood—all in the name of the new Democracy and for the safety of the glorious, free Republic of these United States.

The half-baked radicals, their hearts as soft as their heads, now stand aghast at this terrible sight. They had helped to win the war. Some had sacrificed fathers, brothers, husbands—all of them had suffered an agony of misery and tears, to help the cause of humanity, to make the world safe for democracy. Is *this* what we fought and bled for? they are asking. Have we been misled by the fine-sounding phrases of a Professor, and have we in turn helped to delude the people, the suffering masses of the world? Is the great prophet of the New Democracy strong only in rhetoric?

Pity the mind that awaits miracles and looks expectantly to a universal Savior. The clear-sighted man, well informed, may reasonably foresee the inevitability of certain results from given causes. But only a charlatan can play the great Savior, and only the fool has faith in him. Individuals, however great, may profoundly influence, but are powerless to control, the fate of mankind. Deep socio-political causes produced the war. The Kaiser did not create it, though the spirit of Prussianism no doubt accelerated its coming. Nor is President Wilson responsible for the present bloody peace. He did not make the war: he was made by it. He did not make the peace: he was unmade by it. The social and economic forces that control the world are stronger than any man, than any set of men. These forces are inherent in the fundamental institutions of our wage-slave civilization, in the social atmosphere created by it, and in the individual mind. These forces are by no means harmonious. The human heart and mind, eternally reaching out for greater joy and beauty—the spirit of idealism, in short—is constantly at strife with the established, the institutionalized. These contending social and human factors produce war, as they produce revolution.

The powers that succeeded in turning the instinctive current of man's idealism into the channels of war, became the masters of human destiny for the nonce. By a campaign of publicity and advertising on a scale history had never witnessed before, by chicanery and lying, by exaggeration and misrepresentation, by persistent and long-continued appeals to the basest as well as to the noblest traits of man, by every imaginable and unprecedented manner and method, the great financial interests, eager for war and aided by the international Junkers, thrust humanity into the great world war. Whatever of noble impulse and unsophisticated patriotism there was in the hearts of the masses, in and out of uniform, was soon almost totally drained in the fearsome rivers of human blood, in the brutal, filthy, degrading charnel house of elemental passions set on fire. But the tiger in man, once thoroughly awakened, grew strong and more vicious with the sights he witnessed and the food he was fed on. The basest propensities unchained, the anti-social tendencies engendered and encouraged by the war, and the war propaganda, are now let loose upon the country. Hatred, intolerance, persecution and suppression—the efficient "educational" factors in the preparedness and war campaign—are now permeating the very heart of this country and propagating its virulent poison into every phase of our social life.

But there is no more "Hun" to be hated and lynched. Commerce and business know their interests. We must feed Germany—at a good profit. We must do business with its people. Exit the Hun—*der Moor hat seine Schuldigkeit gethan*. What a significant side-light on the artificiality and life-brevity of national and racial antagonisms, when the fires of mutual distrust and hatred are not fed by the interested stokers of business and religion! But the Frankenstein and intolerance and suppression cultivated by the war campaign is there, alive and vital, and must find some vent for his accumulated bitterness and misery.

Oh, there, the radical, the Bolshevik! What better prey to be cast to the Frankenstein monster?

The powers that be—the plutocratic imperialist and the jingo-profiteer—all heave a happy sigh of relief.

III

The after-war conditions in the United States are filling the Government and the more intelligent, class-conscious capitalists with trepidation. Revolution is stalking across Europe. Its spectre is threatening America. Disquieting signs multiply daily. A new discontent, boding ill and full of terrible possibilities, is manifest in every walk of life. The war has satisfied no one. Only too obviously the glorious promises failed of fulfilment. Excepting the great financial interests and some smaller war profiteers, the American people at large are aching with a poignant disappointment. Some vaguely, other more consciously and clearly, but almost all feel themselves in some way victimized. They had brought supreme sacrifices, suffered untold misery and pain, in the confident hope of a great change to come into their lives after the victorious war, in the assurance of a radically changed and bettered world.

The people feel cheated. Not yet have they been able to fix their gaze definitely upon the specific source of their disappointments, to define the true causes of their discontent. But their impatience with existing conditions is passionate and bitter, and their former faith in the established order profoundly shaken. Significant symptoms of a social breakdown!

Revolutions begin in the heart and in the mind. Action follows in due course. Political and industrial institutions, bereft of the people's faith in them, are doomed. The changed attitude toward the once honored and sacred conditions, now evident throughout the land, symbolizes the complete bankruptcy of the existing order. The old conceptions and ideas underlying present-day society are fast disintegrating. New ideals are germinating in the hearts of the masses—a prolific soil, rich with the promise of a brighter future. America is on the threshold of the Social Revolution.

All this is well realized by the financial and political masters of this country. The situation is profoundly disquieting. But most terrifying to them is the new attitude of labor. It is unprecedented, intolerable in its complete disregard of long accepted standards and conditions, its open rebellion against Things as They Are, its "shameless demands," its defiance of constituted authority. Is it possible, the masters wonder, that we had gone too far in our war-time promises of democracy and freedom, of justice to the workers, of well-being for all? Too reckless was our motto, "Labor will win the war": it has given the toilers a sense of their power, it has made them arrogant, aye, menacing. No more are they satisfied with "a fair day's wage for a fair day's work"; no, not even with wages doubled and trebled. They are laying sacrilegious hands upon the most sacrosanct institution of private ownership, they challenge the exclusive mastery of the owner in his own mine and mill, they demand actual participation in industry, even in the most secret councils that control production and manipulate distribution,— aye, they even dare suggest the taking over by labor of all industry.

Unheard of impudence! Yet this is not all. More menacing still is the revolutionary spirit that is beginning to transfuse itself through every rank of labor, from the highest-paid to the lowest, organized and the unorganized as well. Disobedience is rampant. Gone is the good old respect for orders, the will of superiors is secretly thwarted or openly defied, the mystic power of contracts has lost its old hold. Labor is in rebellion—in rebellion against State and Capital, aye, even against their own leaders that have so long held them in check.

No time is to be lost! Quick, drastic action is necessary. Else the brewing storm will overwhelm us, and the workers deprive us of the wealth we have been at such pains to accumulate. Even now there are such terribly disquieting rumblings, as if the very earth were shaking beneath our feet— rumors of "the dictatorship of the proletariat," of "Soviets of workers, soldiers and sailors." Horrible thought! Why, if the soldiers *should* join these discontented workers, what would become of us poor capitalists? Indeed, have not the police of Boston already set the precedent—made common cause with labor, these traitors to their masters!

"Soviet of Workers," dictatorship of the Proletariat! Why, that's the Russian idea, the terrible Bolshevik menace. Never shall this, the most heinous crime, be forgiven Soviet Russia! Readily would we overlook their repudiation of the Czar's numerous obligations and even their refusal to pay their debts to the American and European money lenders. We'd find some way to recuperate our losses, at a reasonable profit, maybe. But that they have broken down the very pillars of capitalism, abolished profits, given to the peasants the masters' lands for cultivation and use, proclaimed all wealth common property, and subjected the aristocrat and capitalist to the indignity of working for a living—this hellish arch-crime they shall never be forgiven.

That such things should threaten the rich men of this free country is intolerable. Nothing must be left undone to prevent such a calamity. It would be terrible to be put on a level with the common laborer, and we with all our millions unable to procure champagne, because, forsooth, some hod-carrier's brat—illegitimate, perchance—did not get his milk for breakfast. Unthinkable! That is chaos, anarchy! We must not permit our beloved country to come to such a pass. Labor rebellion and discontent must be crushed, energetically, forthwith. Bolsheviki ways and Soviet ideas must gain no foothold in America. But the thing must be done diplomatically; the workers must not be permitted to look into our cards. We should be strong as a lion, subtle as the snake.

IV

The war-time anti-Hun propaganda is now directed against the "Bolshevik," "the radical," and particularly against the Slav or anything resembling him. The man or woman of Russian birth or nationality is made the especial target. The press, the pulpit, all the servile tools of capitalism and imperialism combine to paint Russia, Soviet Russia, in colors of blood and infamy. No misrepresentation, no lie too base to be flung at Russia. Falsehood and forgery the weapons where guns and bayonets have failed. The direct result of this poison propaganda is now culminating in American pogroms against Russians, Bolsheviki, communists, radicals, and progressives in general.

The United States has fortunately always been free from the vicious spirit of race hatred and persecution of the foreigner. The native negro excepted, this country has known no race problem. The American people were never guilty of harboring bitterness or deep-seated prejudice against members of other nationalities. In truth, the great majority of them are themselves of foreign birth or descent, the only true native being the American Indian. Whatever racial differences there may exist between the various nationalities or stocks, they have never assumed the form of active strife. On the contrary, they have always been of a superficial nature, due to misunderstanding or other temporary causes, and have never manifested themselves in anything save light, good-humored banter. Even the much-advertised antagonism of the West toward the Chinese and Japanese is not due to any inherent hatred, but rather to very definite commercial and industrial factors. In the case of the Russians especially, as well as in regard to members of the various branches of the Slavic race, the people of America have always been particularly friendly and well-disposed. But suddenly all the war-time hatred toward the "Hun enemy," the blindest intolerance and persecution are poured upon the head of the Russian, the Slav. Great indeed is the power of propaganda! Great is the power of the American thought controller—the capitalist press. The Russian has become the victim of American pogroms!

Often and again in the past have we Anarchists pointed out that the feudal lords of this land would follow, in their march to imperialism, in the footsteps of the Czars of old Russia, and even outdo their preceptors. Our liberal friends denounced us as fanatics, alarmists, and pessimists. Yet now we are confronted with a state of affairs in democratic America which, in point of brutality and utter repudiation of every fundamental libertarian principle, surpasses the worst autocratic methods the Czars of Russia ever dared apply against political dissenters.

The world is familiar with the story of the pogrom horrors practiced upon the Jews of Czarist Russia. But what the world, especially the American world, does not know is that every pogrom in Russia was directly incited, financed, and prepared by the Government as a means of distracting the attention of the Russian people from the corrupt despotic regime under which they suffered—a deliberate method of confusing and checking the fast growing discontent and holding back the rising tide of revolutionary upheaval.

But thoughtful people in Russia were not long deceived by this hellish stratagem. That is why Russians of character and intelligence never lent themselves to the practice of Jew-baiting and persecution. The authorities frequently had to resort to importing the human dregs of distant communities, fill them with vodka, and then turn them loose on the defenceless Jews. These Black Hundreds and hooligans of Czarist Russia were the infamous regime now forever cast into the abyss of oblivion by the awakened and regenerated spirit of New Russia. There have been no pogroms in Soviet Russia.

But the Black Hundreds and the hooligans have now come to life again—in democratic America. Here they are more mad and pernicious than their Russian colleagues in crime had ever been. Their wild orgies of assault and destruction are directed, not against the Jew, but against the more comprehensive scape-goat of Capitalism, "the alien," the "radical." These are being made the lightning rod upon which is to be drawn all the fury of the storm that is menacing the American plutocracy. As the Czars pointed at the Jew as the sole source and cause of the Russian people's poverty and servitude, so the feudal lords of America have chosen the "foreign radical," "the Bolshevik" as the vicarious victim for the sins of the capitalist order. But while no intelligent and self-respecting Russian ever degraded himself with the Czar's bloody work, we see in our democracy so-called cultured people, professional men and women, "good Americans," inspired and aided by the "respectable, reputable" press, turn into bestial mobs. We see high Government officials, State and Federal, play the part of the hooligans, encouraging and aiding the American Black Hundred of legionaries, in a frenzied crusade against the "foreigner," whose sole crime consists in taking seriously the American guarantees of free speech, free press, and free assembly.

The war hate against everything German was vicious enough, though the people of America were repeatedly assured that we were not making war against the German people. One can understand also, though not countenance, the vulgar clamor against the best and finest expressions of German culture, the stupid prohibition of the language of Goethe and Schiller, of the revolutionary music of Wagner and Beethoven, the poetry of Heine, the writings of Nietzsche, and all the other great creative works of Teuton genius. But what possible reason is there for the post-war hatred toward aliens in general and Russians in particular? The outrages and cruelties perpetrated upon Germans in America during the war pale almost into insignificance compared with the horrible treatment the Russians in the United States are now subjected to. In fact, the Czarist pogroms, barring a few exceptions, never rivaled the fearful excesses now happening almost daily in various American cities, their victims, men and women, guilty only of being Russians.

This state of affairs is the more significant because Russians, and the Slavic people in general, were hitherto always welcomed to these shores as the best offering Europe contributed to the Moloch of American industry. The Slav was so good natured, and docile, such a patient slave, so appreciative of the liberties he enjoyed in the new land—"liberties" which the socially conscious American had long since learned to see as a delusion and a snare. But to the unsophisticated Russian peasant, always half-starved and browbeaten, they seemed real and resplendant, the symbol of paradise found. By the thousands he flocked to the promised land, swarmed into the centers of industry to build our railroads, forge iron, dig coal, till the soil, weave cloth, and toil at scores of other useful occupations, his reward a mere pittance.

Nor was it only the workers in fields and factories who were welcomed here from Russia. Russian culture was an honored guest in America. The great literature of the Slav, his music, his dancing—all found the most generous reception and fullest appreciation. Above all, the Russian *intelligentzia*, the political refugees, exiles, and active revolutionists that came to America, and came—most of them—not merely to express their opinions but rather to plot the forcible overthrow of the Russian autocracy, all found sympathetic hearing and generous purses in this country, aye, even at the seat of Government.

And now? Now it is considered the most heinous crime to have been born in Russia.

What has caused this peculiar change? What is back of this sudden reversal of feeling?

It is the Russian Revolution. Not, of course, the Miliukov-Kerensky revolution, but the real revolution that gave birth to Soviet Russia. The submissive, enslaved, long-suffering Russian people unexpectedly transformed into a free, daring Giant breaking a new path for the progress of mankind—that is the reason for the changed attitude of the capitalistic world. It is one thing to help Russian revolutionists to overthrow the Czar and to put in his place a "democratic" form of government which has proven such a boon to our own Czars of commerce and industry. But it is quite a different thing to see the Prometheus of labor rise in his might, strike off his chains, and with the full consciousness of his complete economic power bring to life the dreams and aspirations of a thousand years,—the economic, political, and spiritual emancipation of the masses of the world. This pioneer social experiment now being tried in Russia—the greatest and most fundamental ever witnessed in all history—is the guiding star to all the oppressed and disinherited of the world. Already its magic light is spreading over the whole European horizon, the harbinger of the approaching Dawn of Man. What if it should traverse the ocean and embrace our own shores within its orbit? The whole social order of the financial Czars, industrial Kaisers, and land Barons of America is at stake: the "order" maintained by club and gun, by jail and lynch law in and out of court; the "order" founded on robbery and violence, built upon sham and unreason, artificiality and insanity, and supported by misery and starvation, by the water-cure, the dungeon and straitjacket; an "order" that transcends all chaos and daily makes confusion worse confounded.

Such social "order" is doomed. It bears within itself the virus of disintegration. Already the conscience of America is awakening. The war marked the crisis. Already American men have chosen imprisonment, torture, and death, rather than become participants in an unholy war. Already American men and women are beginning to realize the anti-social destructive character and purpose of authority and government by violence, force, and fraud. Already the workers of America are outgrowing the vicious circle of craft-unionism, learning the lesson and the power of solidarity of the international proletariat, and gaining confidence in their own initiative and judgment, to the confusion and terror of their antiquated, spineless leadership. Already they are seeing through the sham of "equality before the law," and are in open rebellion to government by injunction.

A spark from the glowing flame of Soviet Russia, and the purse-proud autocracy of America may be swept away by the social conflagration.

Wherefore the united chorus of all Czars and Kaisers, "Death to the Bolsheviki, the aliens, the I. W. Ws., the Communists, the Anarchists!"

V

Whatever might be said of the American plutocracy and the Government, no one can accuse them of originality. The methods used by them to confuse and confound the people are but cheap imitations of the old tactics long resorted to by the despotic rulers of Europe. Even before the world war Washington had borrowed many a trick from London. And all through the war American militarism, with its conscription, espionage, torture of conscientious objectors, and suppressive legislation, was but aping—stupidly and destructively—the *modus operandi* of the bankrupt imperialism of the Old World. For lack of originality and ideas, American officialdom was content to be the echo of the military and court circles of London and Paris. And now again we witness Washington following in the exact footsteps of the worst autocracy of modern times. For the hue and cry against the "alien" is a faithful replica of the persecution of the Jews by the Czars of Russia, and the American pogroms against radicals are the exaggerated picture of Russian Jew-baiting.

And, finally, the most infamous and most inhuman method of Czarist Russia, the method that sacrificed hundreds of thousands of the finest and bravest men and women of Russia, and systematically robbed the country of the very flower of its youth, is now being transplanted on American soil, in these great United States, the freest democracy on earth. The dreaded

Russian *administrative process* the newest American institutions! Sudden seizure, anonymous denunciation, star chamber proceedings, the third degree, secret deportation and banishment to unknown lands. O shades of Jefferson, Thomas Paine, and Patrick Henry! That you must witness the bloodiest weapon of Czarism rescued from the ruins of defunct absolutism and introduced into the country for whose freedom you had fought so heroically!

What means the administrative process?

It means the suppression and elimination of the political protestant and social rebel. It is the practice of picking men upon the street, on the merest suspicion of "political untrustworthiness," of arresting them in their club rooms or homes, tearing them away from their families, locking them up in jails or detention pens, holding them *incommunicado* for weeks and months, depriving them of a hearing in open court, denying them trial by jury, and finally deporting them or banishing them to unknown shores. All this, not for any crime committed or even any punishable act charged, but merely on the denunciation of an enemy or the irresponsible accusation by a Secret Service man that the "suspect" holds certain unpopular or "forbidden" opinions.

Lest the truth or accuracy of this statement be called in question, let it be stated that at this very moment there are one hundred such "political suspects" held at Ellis Island, with several hundred more in the various Immigration Detention jails, every one of them a victim of the administrative process described above. Not one of them is charged with any specific crime; one and all are accused of entertaining "illegal" views on political or Social questions. Nearly all of them have been seized on the street or arrested in their homes or reading-rooms while engaged in the dangerous pursuit of studying the English language, mathematics, or American history. (The latter seems lately to be regarded by the authorities as a particularly dangerous occupation, and those guilty of it a *prima facie* menace to our American institutions.) Others were arrested in the factory, at their work bench, or in the numerous recent raids of homes and peaceful meetings. Many of them were beaten and clubbed most brutally, the wounds of some necessitating hospital treatment. In the police stations they were subjected to the third degree, threatened, tortured, and finally thrust into the bull pens of Ellis Island. Here they are treated as dangerous felons, kept all the time under lock and key, and allowed to see their wives and families only once a week, with a screen between them and malicious guards constantly at their side. Here their mail is subjected to the most stringent censorship, and their letters delivered or not, according to the whims of the petty officials in charge. Here some of them, because they dared protest against their isolation and the putrid food, were placed in the insane asylum. Here it was that the brutal treatment and unbearable conditions of existence drove men and women, the politicals awaiting deportation, to the desperate extremity of a hunger strike, the last resort of defenseless beings, the paradoxical self-defense of despair. For weeks and months these men have now been kept prisoners at Ellis Island, tortured by the thought of their wives and children whom the Government has ruthlessly deprived of support, and living in constant uncertainty of the fate that is awaiting them, for the good American Government, refinedly cruel, is keeping their destination secret, and certain death may be the goal of the deportees when the hour of departure finally strikes.

Such is the treatment and the fate of the first group of Russian refugees from American "democracy." Such is the process known as the administrative methods, penalizing governmentally unapproved Thought, suppressing *disbelief* in the omniscience of the powers that be.

In enlightened, free America. Not in Darkest Russia.

When the terrible significance of the administrative process practiced in Russia became known in Europe, civilization stood aghast. It caused a storm of protest in the British Parliament, and called forth violent interpellations in the Italian Diet and the French Chamber. Even the German Reichstag, in the days of the omnipotent Kaiser, ventured a heated debate of the barbaric administrative process which doomed thousands of innocents to underground dungeons and the frozen *taigas* of Siberia.

Are the Czar's methods, the Third Section, the secret political spy organizations, anonymous denunciations, star chamber proceedings, deprivation of trial, wholesale deportations and banishment, to become an established American institution? Let the people speak.

The full significance of the principle of deportation is becoming daily more apparent. The field of its menace is progressively broadening. Not only the alien social rebel is to be crushed by the new White Terror. Its hand is already reaching out far for the naturalized American whose social views are frowned upon by the Government. And yet deeper it strikes. One hundred per cent Americanism is to root out the last vestige, the very memory, of traditional American freedom. Not alone foreigners, but the naturalized citizen and the native-born are to be mentally fumigated, made politically "reliable" and governmentally *kosher*, by eliminating the social critics and industrial protestants, by denaturalization and banishment, by exile to the Island of Guam or to Alaska, the future Siberia of the United States.

Following the "alien radical," the naturalized American is the first victim of the Czarification of America. Patriotic profiteers and political hooligans are united in the cry for the "Americanization" of the foreigner in the United States. He is to be "naturalized," intellectually sterilized and immunized to Bolshevism, so that he may properly appreciate the glorious spirit of American democracy. Simultaneously, however, the Federal Government is introducing the new policy of summarily depriving the naturalized American of his citizenship, in order to bring him when so desired, within the scope of the administrative process which subjects the victim to deportation without trial.

A most important precedent had already been set. The case of Emma Goldman affords significant proof to what lengths the Government will go to rid itself of a disquieting social rebel, though he be a citizen for a quarter of a century.

The story is interesting and enlightening. More than eight years ago Secret Service men of the Federal Government were ordered to gather "material" in Rochester, N. Y., or elsewhere, that would enable the authorities to disfranchise a certain Rochester citizen. The man in question was of no concern whatever to Washington, as subsequent events proved. He was an ordinary citizen, a quiet working man, without any interest in social or political questions. He was never known to entertain any unpopular views or opinions. As a matter of fact, the man had long been considered dead by his local friends and acquaintances; since he had disappeared from his home years previously and no clue to his whereabouts or any sign that he was still among the living could be found; indeed, has not been found till this day, notwithstanding the best efforts. At great expense, and with considerable winking at its own rules and regulations in such matters, the United States Government finally disfranchised the man—the corpse, perhaps, for anything known to the contrary. The proceeding necessitated a good deal of secrecy and subterfuge, for even the wife of the man in question, whose status as citizen by right of her marriage was involved, was not apprised by the Government of its intended action. On the pretext that the man was not fully of legal age at the time of his naturalization—about 20 years before—the mighty Republic of America declared the citizenship of the man of unknown whereabouts and against whom no crime or offence of any kind was ever charged, as null and void.

Ten years passed. The disfranchised citizen, so far as humanly known, was still as dead as at the time of his denaturalization. No trace of him could be found, and nothing more was heard of the motives and purposes of the Government in depriving of citizenship a man who had apparently been dead for years. Dark and peculiar are the ways of Government.

More time passed. Then it became known that the United States Government intended to deport Emma Goldman. But Emma Goldman had acquired citizenship by marriage 30 years before, and, as a citizen, she could not be deported under the present laws of the United States. But lo and behold! The Government suddenly announced that Emma Goldman was a citizen no more, because her husband had been disfranchised ten years ago!

Dark and peculiar indeed are the ways of government. But there is method in its madness.

What a striking comment this case affords on the true character of government, and the chicanery and subterfuge it resorts to when legal means fail to achieve its purposes. Long did the United States Government bide its time. The moment was not propitious to get rid of Emma Goldman. But she must be gotten rid of, by fair means or foul. Yet public sentiment was not ready for such things as deportation and banishment. Patience! The hour of a great popular hysteria will come, will be made, if necessary, and then we shall deport this *bete noir* of government.

The moment has now come. It is here. The national hysteria against radicals, inspired and fed by the bourgeois press, pulpit, and politicians, has created the atmosphere needed to introduce in America the principle and practice of banishment. At last the Government may deport Emma Goldman, for through the width and breadth of the country there is not a Judge—and possibly not even a jury—with enough integrity and courage to give this *enfant terrible* a fair hearing and an unprejudiced examination of her claim to citizenship.

Therefore Emma Goldman is to be deported.

But her case sets a precedent, and American life is ruled by legal precedents. Henceforth the naturalized citizen may be disfranchised, on one pretext or another, and deported because of his or her social views and opinions. Already Congress is preparing to embody this worthy precedent in our national legislation by passing special laws providing for the disenfranchisement of naturalized Americans for reasons satisfactory to our autocratic regime.

Thus another link is forged to chain the great American people. For it is against the liberties and welfare of the people at large that these new methods are fundamentally directed. Not merely against Emma Goldman, the Anarchists, the I. W. Ws., Communists, and other revolutionists. These are but the primary victims, the prologue which introduces and shadows forth the tragedy about to be enacted.

The ultimate blow of the imperialist plutocracy of America is aimed at Labor, at the increasing discontent of the masses, their growing class-consciousness, and their progressive aspiration for more joy and life and beauty. The fate of America is in the balance.

That is the true meaning and the real menace of the principle of deportation, banishment, and exile, now being introduced in the life of the United States. That is the purpose of the State and Federal Anti-Anarchist laws, criminal-syndicalist-legislation, and all similar weapons that the master class is forging for the defeat of the awakening proletariat of America.

Shall the United States, once the land of opportunity, the refuge of all the oppressed, be Prussianized, Czarified? Shall the melting pot of the world be turned into a fiery caldron brewing strife and slaughter, spitting tyranny and assassination? Shall we here, on this soil baptized with the sacred blood of the great heroes of the Revolutionary War, engage in the sanguinary struggle of brother against brother? Shall we re-enact in this land the frightful nightmare of Darkest Russia? Shall this land re-echo the horrible tramp, tramp of a thousand feet, on their way to an American Siberia? Tortured bodies, manacled hands, clanking chains, in weary, endless procession—shall that be the heritage of our youth? Shall the songs of mothers be turned into a dirge, and little babies be suckled with the teat of hate?

No, it shall not be. There is yet time to pause, to turn back. High time, high time for the voice of every true man and woman, of every lover of liberty, to thunder forth such a mighty collective protest that shall reverberate from North to South, and East to West, and rouse the awakened manhood of America to a heroic stand for Liberty and Justice.

But if not,—if our warning prediction unhappily come true and the fearful tragedy be played to its end, yet shall we not despair, nor misdoubt the *finale*.

Hateful is the Dream of Oppression. And as vain. Where the man who could name the judges that doomed Socrates? Where the persecutors of the Gracchi, the banishers of Aristides, the excommunicators of Spinoza and Tolstoy? Their very memory is obliterated by the footsteps of Progress.

Unceasingly it marches, forward and upward, all obstacles notwithstanding, keeping time with the heart beats of Humanity. Vain the efforts to halt it, to banish ideas, to strangle thought. Vain the frenzied struggle to turn back the hands of Time. The mightiest Goliath of Reaction has fought his last fight—his final gesture, Old Russia, a hopeless surrender. Too late to revive this corpse. It is beyond resurrection. Attempts there may be, aye, will be, for the Bourbons never learn,—and the people are long suffering. But attempts useless, destructive, utterly fatal to their purpose. The Dream of Reaction ends in abysmal nightmare.

It is darkest before dawn, in history as in nature. But the dawn has begun. In Russia. Its light is a promise and the hope of the world.

WHAT'S TO BE DONE?

Men and women of America, there is much work to be done. If you hate injustice and tyranny, if you love liberty and beauty, there is work for you. If oppression rouses your indignation, and the sight of misery and ugliness makes you unhappy, there is work for you. If your country is dear to you and the people your kin, there is work for you. There is much to be done.

Whoever you are, artist or educator, writer or worker—be you but a true man or true woman—there is important work for you. Let not prejudice and narrow-mindedness blind you. Let not a false press mislead you. Permit not this country to sink to the depths of despotism. Do not stand supinely by, while every passing day strengthens reaction. Rouse yourself and others to resent injustice and every outrage on liberty. Demand an open mind and fair hearing for every idea. Hold sacred the right of expression: protect the freedom of speech and press. Suffer not Thought to be forcibly limited and opinions proscribed. Make conscience free, undisciplined. Allow no curtailment of aspirations and ideals. These are the levers of progress, the fountain-head of joy and beauty.

Join your efforts, lovers of humanity. Do not uphold the hand that strangles Life. Align yourselves with the dreamers of the Better Day. The cause is worthy, the need urgent. The future looks towards you, its voice calls you, calls.

May it not call in vain.

And you, fellow workers in factory, mine, and field, a great mission is yours. You, the feeders of the world and the creators of its wealth, you are the most interested in the fate of your country. The menace of despotism is greatest to you. Long has your masters' service humiliated and degraded you. Will you permit yourselves to be driven into still more abject slavery? Your emancipation is *your* work. Others may help, but you alone can win. In shop and union, take up this your greatest problem. Let not the least of you be victimized. Remember, an injury to one is the concern of all. No worker can stand alone in the face of organized capitalism with all its legislative and military weapons. Learn solidarity: each with a common purpose, all with a common effort. Know your enemy: there is no "mutual interest" between the robber and the robbed. Understand your true friends. You'll always find them maligned and persecuted by *your* enemies. The idealists, the seekers of the slaveless world, speak from *your* heart. Give them hearing.

Your fate, the fate of the country, is in *your* hands. Yours is the mightiest power. There is no strength in the Government, except you give it. No strength in your masters, except you suffer it. The only true mastery is in you, the working class, in your power to feed and clothe the world and make it joyous. The greatest power, for good or evil. Use it for liberty, for justice. Allow no suppression of the freedom of thought and speech, for it is a snare for *your* undoing. Sooner or later every suppression comes home to labor, for its greater enslavement. Realize the menace of deportation, of the principle of banishment and exile. 'Tis the latest method of the American plutocracy to silence the discontent of the workers. Lose no time. It is of the most vital importance to you. It threatens you, your union, your very existence. Take the matter up in your organizations. The fortunes of labor in America are at stake. Only your united effort can conquer the peril that menaces you. Take action. Rouse the workers of the whole country. In union and solidarity, in clear purpose and courage is your only salvation.

Quotations from American and Foreign Authors Which Would Fall Under the Criminal Anarchy Law, Espionage Law, Etc.

These authors, distinguished thinkers, philosophers and humanitarians of world-wide renown would, if still alive and of foreign birth, not be permitted on American shores if they tried to land here, or, if born Americans, they would be threatened by deportation to the Island of Guam.

ABRAHAM LINCOLN

The man who will not investigate both sides of a question is dishonest.

The cause of civil liberty must not be surrendered at the end of one or even one hundred defeats.

The authors of the Declaration of Independence meant it to be a stumbling block to those who in after times might seek to turn free people back into the paths of despotism.

I have always thought that all men should be free, but if any should be slaves, it should be first those who desire it for themselves, and secondly those who desire it for others.

If there is anything that it is the duty of the whole people never to intrust to any hands but their own, that thing is the preservation and perpetuity of their own liberties.

THOMAS JEFFERSON

All eyes are opening to the rights of man. The general spread of the light of science has already laid open to every view the palpable truth, that the mass of mankind has not been born with saddles on their backs, nor a favored few booted and spurred, ready to ride them legitimately, by the grace of God.

Societies exist under three forms, sufficiently distinguishable: (1) Without government, as among our Indians. (2) Under governments wherein the will of every one has a just influence; as is the case in England, in a slight degree, and in our States, in a great one. (3) Under governments of force; as is the case in all other monarchies, and in most of the other republics. To have an idea of the curse of existence under these last, they must be seen. It is a government of wolves over sheep. It is a problem, not clear in my mind, that the first condition is not the best. But I believe it to be inconsistent with any great degree of population. The second state has a great deal of good in it. The mass of mankind under that, enjoys a precious degree of liberty and happiness. It has its evils, too; the principal of which is the turbulence to which it is subject. But weight this against the oppressions of monarchy, and it becomes nothing. Even this evil is productive of good. It prevents the degeneracy of governments, and nourishes a general attention to the public affairs. I hold it, that a little rebellion, now and then, is a good thing, and as necessary in the political world as storms in the physical. Unsuccessful rebellions, indeed, generally establish the encroachments on the rights of the people, which have produced them. An observation of this truth should render honest republican governors so mild in their punishment of rebellions, as not to discourage them too much. It is a medicine necessary for the sound health of governments.

We have long enough suffered under the base prostitution of law to party passions in one judge, and the imbecility of another.

It is error alone which needs the support of government. Truth can stand by itself.

WILLIAM LLOYD GARRISON

Liberty for each, for all, and forever.

No person will rule over me with my consent. I will rule over no man.

Enslave the liberty of but one human being and the liberties of the world are put in peril.

When I look at these crowded thousands, and see them trample on their consciences and the rights of their fellowmen at the bidding of a piece of parchment, I say, my curse be on the Constitution of the United States.

Why, sir, no freedom of speech or inquiry is conceded to me in this land. Am I not vehemently told both at the North and the South that I have no right to meddle with the question of slavery? And my right to speak on any other subject, in opposition to public opinion, is equally denied to me.

I am aware that many object to the severity of my language; but is there not cause for severity? I will be as harsh as Truth, and as uncompromising as Justice. On this subject I do not wish to think, or speak, or write, with moderation. No! No! Tell a man whose house is on fire to give a moderate alarm; tell him to moderately rescue his wife from the hands of the ravisher; tell the mother to gradually extricate her babe from the fire into which it has fallen—but urge me not to use moderation in a cause like the present. I am in earnest—I will not equivocate—I will not excuse—I will not retreat a single inch—and I will be heard. The apathy of the people is enough to make every statue leap from its pedestal and hasten to the resurrection of the dead.—*In the first issue of the Liberator, January 1, 1831.*

WENDELL PHILLIPS

If there is anything that cannot bear free thought, let it crack.

Nothing but Freedom, Justice, and Truth is of any permanent advantage to the mass of mankind. To these society, left to itself, is always tending.

"The right to think, to know and to utter," as John Milton said, is the dearest of all liberties. Without this right, there can be no liberty to any people; with it, there can be no slavery.

When you have convinced thinking men that it is right, and humane men that it is just, you will gain your cause. Men always lose half of what is gained by violence. What is gained by argument, is gained forever.

The manna of liberty must be gathered each day, or it is rotten.

Only by unintermitted agitation can a people be kept sufficiently awake to principle not to let liberty be smothered in material prosperity.

Let us believe that the whole truth can never do harm to the whole of virtue; and remember that in order to get the whole of truth, you must allow every man, right or wrong, freely to utter his conscience, and protect him in so doing. Entire unshackled freedom for every man's life, no matter how wide its range. The community which dares not protect its humblest and most hated member in the free utterance of his opinions, no matter how false or hateful, is only a gang of slaves.

STEPHEN PEARL ANDREWS

Governments have hitherto been established, and have apologized for the unseemly fact of their existence, from the necessity of establishing and maintaining order; but order has never yet been maintained, revolutions and violent outbreaks have never yet been ended, public peace and harmony have never yet been secured, for the precise reason that the organic, essential, and indestructible natures of the objects which it was attempted to reduce to order have always been constricted and infringed by every such attempt. Just in proportion as the effort is less and less made to reduce men to order, just in that proportion they become more orderly, as witness the difference in the state of society in Austria and the United States. Plant an army of one hundred thousand soldiers in New York, as at Paris, to preserve the peace, and we should have a bloody revolution in a week; and be assured that the only remedy for what little of turbulence remains among us, as compared with European societies, will be found to be more liberty. When there remain positively no external restrictions, there will be positively no disturbance, provided always certain regulating principles of justice, to which I shall advert presently, are accepted and enter into the public mind, serving as substitutes for every species of repressive laws.

HENRY GEORGE

In our time, as in times before, creep on the insidious forces that, producing inequality, destroy Liberty. On the horizon the clouds begin to lower. Liberty calls to us again. We must follow her further; we must trust her fully. Either we must wholly accept her or she will not stay. It is not enough that men should vote; it is not enough that they should be theoretically equal before the law. They must have liberty to avail themselves of the opportunities and means of life; they must stand on equal terms with reference to the bounty of nature. Either this, or Liberty withdraws her light! Either this, or darkness comes on, and the very forces that progress has evolved turn to powers that work destruction. This is the universal law. This is the lesson of the centuries. Unless its foundations be laid in justice the social structure cannot stand.

HENRY DAVID THOREAU

Law never made men a whit more just; and, by means of their respect for it, even the well-disposed are daily made the agents of injustice. A common and natural result of an undue respect for law is that you may see a file of soldiers, colonel, captain, corporal, privates, powder-monkeys, and all, marching in admirable order over hill and dale to the wars, against their wills, aye, against their common sense and consciences, which makes it very steep marching indeed, and produces a palpitation of the heart. They have no doubt that it is a damnable business in which they are concerned; they are all peaceably inclined. Now, what are they? Men at all? or small movable forts and magazines, at the service of some unscrupulous man in power?

The mass of men serve the State thus, not as men mainly, but as machines, with their bodies. They are the standing army, and the militia, gaolers, constables, posse comitatus, etc. In most cases there is no free exercise whatever of the judgment or of the moral sense; but they put themselves on a level with wood and earth and stones; and wooden men can perhaps be manufactured that will serve the purpose as well. Such command no more respect than men of straw or a lump of dirt. They have the same sort of worth only as horses and dogs. Yet such as these even are commonly esteemed good citizens.

Others—as most legislators, politicians, lawyers, ministers, and office-holders—serve the State chiefly with their heads; and as they rarely make any moral distinctions, they are as likely to serve the devil, without *intending* it, as God.

How does it become a man to behave toward this American government today? I answer, that he cannot without disgrace, be associated with it. I cannot for an instant recognize that political organization as *my* government which is the *slave's* government also.

All men recognize the right of revolution; that is, the right to refuse allegiance to, and to resist, the government, when its tyranny or its inefficiency are great and unendurable.

RALPH WALDO EMERSON

It will never make any difference to a hero what the laws are.

> For what avail the plough or sail
>
> Or land or life, if freedom fail?

The wise know that foolish legislation is a rope of sand which perishes in the twisting.

Our distrust is very expensive. The money we spend for courts and prisons is very ill laid out.

Every actual State is corrupt. Good men must not obey the laws too well. What satire on government can equal the severity of censure conveyed in the word *politics* which now for ages has signified *cunning*, intimating that the State is a trick?

No law can be sacred to me but that of my nature. Good and bad are but names very readily transferable to that or this; the only right is what is after my constitution, the only wrong what is against it. A man is to carry himself in the presence of all opposition, as if everything were titular and ephemeral but him. I am ashamed to think how easily we capitulate to badges and names, to large societies and dead institutions.

EDMUND BURKE

All writers on the science of policy are agreed, and they agree with experience, that all governments must frequently infringe the rules of justice to support themselves; that truth must give way to dissimulation, honesty to convenience, and humanity to the reigning interest. The whole of this mystery of iniquity is called the reason of state. It is a reason which I own I cannot penetrate. What sort of a protection is this of the general right, that is maintained by infringing the rights of particulars? What sort of justice is this which is enforced by breaches of its own laws? These paradoxes I leave to be solved by the able heads of legislators and politicians. For my part, I say what a plain man would say on such occasion. I can never believe that any institution, agreeable to nature, and proper for mankind, could find it necessary, or even expedient, in any case whatsoever, to do what the best and worthiest instinct of mankind warn us to avoid. But no wonder that what is set up in opposition to the state of nature should preserve itself by trampling upon the law of nature.

THOMAS PAINE

To argue with a man who has renounced his reason is like giving medicine to the dead.

The more perfect civilization is, the less occasion has it for government, because the more does it regulate its own affairs, and govern itself; but so contrary is the practice of old governments to the reason of the case, that the expenses of them increase in the proportion they ought to diminish. It is but few general laws that civilized life requires, and those of such common usefulness, that whether they are enforced by the forms of government or not, the effect will be nearly the same. If we consider what the principles are that first condense men into society, and what the motives that regulate their mutual intercourse afterwards, we shall find, by the time we arrive at what is called government, that nearly the whole of the business is performed by the natural operation of the parts upon each other.

Society in every state is a blessing, but government, even in its best state, is but a necessary evil; in its worst state, an intolerable one.

The trade of governing has always been monopolized by the most ignorant and the most rascally individuals of mankind.

JOHN STUART MILL

Mankind can hardly be too often reminded, that there was once a man named Socrates, between whom and the legal authorities and public opinion of his time, there took place a memorable collision. Born in an age and country abounding in individual greatness, this man has been handed down to us by those who best knew both him and the age, as the most virtuous man in it; while we know him as the head and prototype of all subsequent teachers of virtue, the source equally of the lofty inspiration of Plato and the judicious utilitarianism of Aristotle, the two headsprings of ethical as of all other philosophy. Their acknowledged master of all the eminent thinkers who have since lived—whose fame, still growing after more than two thousand years, all but outweighs the whole remainder of the names which make his native city illustrious—was put to death by his countrymen, after a judicial conviction, for impiety and immorality. Impiety, in denying the Gods recognized by the State; indeed his accusers asserted (see the "Apologia") that he believed in no gods at all. Immorality, in being, by his doctrines and instructions, a "corrupter of youth." Of these charges the tribunal, there is every ground for believing, honestly found him guilty, and condemned the man who probably of all then born had deserved best of mankind, to be put to death as a criminal.

HERBERT SPENCER

When we have made our constitution purely democratic, thinks to himself the earnest reformer, we shall have brought government into harmony with absolute justice. Such a faith, though perhaps needful for the age, is a very erroneous one. By no process can coercion be made equitable. The freest form of government is only the least objectionable form. The rule of the many by the few we call tyranny: the rule of the few by the many is tyranny also, only of a less intense kind. "You shall do as we will, and not as you will," is in either case the declaration; and, if the hundred make it to ninety-nine instead of the ninety-nine to the hundred, it is only a fraction less immoral. Of two such parties, whichever fulfills this declaration, necessarily breaks the law of equal freedom: the only difference being that by the one it is broken in the persons of ninety-nine, whilst by the other it is broken in the persons of a hundred. And the merit of the democratic form of government consists solely in this,—that it trespasses against the smallest number.

The very existence of majorities and minorities is indicative of an immoral state. The man whose character harmonizes with the moral law, we found to be one who can obtain complete happiness without establishing the happiness of his fellows. But the enactment of public arrangements by vote implies a society consisting of men otherwise constituted—implies that the desires of some cannot be satisfied without sacrificing the desires of others—implies that in the pursuit of their happiness the majority inflict a certain amount of *un*happiness on the minority—implies, therefore, organic immorality. Thus, from another point of view, we again perceive that even in its most equitable form it is impossible for government to disassociate itself from evil; and further, that, unless the right to ignore the State is recognized, its acts must be essentially criminal.

LYOF N. TOLSTOY

The cause of the miserable condition of the workers is slavery. The cause of slavery is legislation. Legislation rests on organized violence. It follows that an improvement in the condition of the people is possible only through the abolition of organized violence. "But organized violence is government, and how can we live without governments? Without governments there will be chaos, anarchy; all the achievements of civilization will perish, and the people will revert to their primitive barbarism." But why should we suppose this? Why think that non-official people could not arrange it, not for themselves, but for others? We see, on the contrary, that in the most diverse matters people in our times arrange their own lives incomparably better than those who govern them arrange for them. Without the least help from government, and often in spite of the interference of government, people organize all sorts of social undertakings—workmen's unions, co-operative societies, railway companies, and syndicates. If collections for public works are needed, why should we suppose that free people could not without violence voluntarily collect the necessary means, and carry out all that is carried out by means of taxes, if only the undertakings in question are really useful for anybody? Why suppose that there cannot be tribunals without violence?

The robber generally plundered the rich, the governments generally plunder the poor and protect those rich who assist in their crimes. The robber doing his work risked his life, while the governments risk nothing, but base their whole activity on lies and deception. The robber did not compel anyone to join his band, the governments generally enrol their soldiers by force. All who paid the tax to the robber had equal security from danger. But in the state, the more any one takes part in the organized fraud the more he receives not merely of protection, but also of reward.